oasis

The Chord Songbook

Wise Publications
London/New York/Paris/Sydney/Copenhagen/Madrid

Exclusive Distributors:
Music Sales Limited
8/9 Frith Street,
London W1V 5TZ, England.
Music Sales Pty Limited
120 Rothschild Avenue,
Rosebery, NSW 2018, Australia.

Order No. AM936903
ISBN 0-7119-5735-5
This book © Copyright 1996 by Wise Publications

Compiled by Peter Evans
Music arranged by Howard Johnstone
Music processed by The Pitts

Cover design by Pearce Marchbank, Studio Twenty
Quarked by Ben May
Cover photograph by London Features International

Printed in the United Kingdom by
Caligraving Limited, Thetford, Norfolk.

Your Guarantee of Quality
As publishers, we strive to produce every book
to the highest commercial standards.
This book has been carefully designed to minimise awkward
page turns and to make playing from it a real pleasure.
Particular care has been given to specifying acid-free,
neutral-sized paper made from pulps which have not been
elemental chlorine bleached. This pulp is from farmed sustainable
forests and was produced with special regard for the environment.
Throughout, the printing and binding have been planned to
ensure a sturdy, attractive publication which should give years
of enjoyment. If your copy fails to meet our high standards,
please inform us and we will gladly replace it.

Music Sales' complete catalogue describes thousands
of titles and is available in full colour sections by subject,
direct from Music Sales Limited. Please state your areas of interest
and send a cheque/postal order for £1.50 for postage to:
Music Sales Limited, Newmarket Road,
Bury St. Edmunds, Suffolk IP33 3YB.

Visit the Internet Music Shop at
http://www.musicsales.co.uk

Relative Tuning

The guitar can be tuned with the aid of pitch pipes or dedicated electronic guitar tuners which are available through your local music dealer. If you do not have a tuning device, you can use relative tuning. Estimate the pitch of the 6th string as near as possible to E or at least a comfortable pitch (not too high, as you might break other strings in tuning up). Then, while checking the various positions on the diagram, place a finger from your left hand on the:

5th fret of the E or 6th string and **tune the open A** (or 5th string) to the note (A)

5th fret of the A or 5th string and **tune the open D** (or 4th string) to the note (D)

5th fret of the D or 4th string and **tune the open G** (or 3rd string) to the note (G)

4th fret of the G or 3rd string and **tune the open B** (or 2nd string) to the note (B)

5th fret of the B or 2nd string and **tune the open E** (or 1st string) to the note (E)

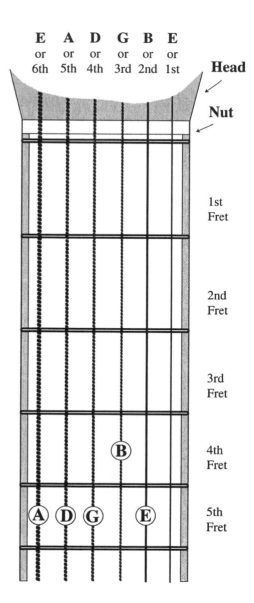

Reading Chord Boxes

Chord boxes are diagrams of the guitar neck viewed head upwards, face on as illustrated. The top horizontal line is the nut, unless a higher fret number is indicated, the others are the frets.

The vertical lines are the strings, starting from E (or 6th) on the left to E (or 1st) on the right.

The black dots indicate where to place your fingers.

Strings marked with an O are played open, not fretted.

Strings marked with an X should not be played.

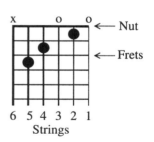

3

Cast No Shadow

Words & Music by
Noel Gallagher

Asus⁴ **G** **Em** **D** **C**

Intro   ‖: Asus⁴ | Asus⁴ | G | G   :‖

Verse 1

Asus⁴
Here's a thought for every man
                                                              G
Who tries to understand what is in his hands.
          Asus⁴
He walks along the open road of love and life
               G
Surviving if he can.
Em   **D**
Bound with all the weight
               C   **G**
Of all the words he tried to say.
Em   **D**
Chained to all the places
               C   **G**
That he never wished to stay.
Em   **D**
Bound with all the weight
               C   **G**
Of all the words he tried to say.
Em   **D**   **C**
As he faced the sun he cast no shadow.

Chorus 1

G   **Asus⁴**   **C** | **Em** **D** |
As they took his soul they stole his pride,
G   **Asus⁴**   **C** | **Em** **D** |
As they took his soul they stole his pride,
G   **Asus⁴**   **C** | **Em** **D** |
As they took his soul they stole his pride,
Em   **D**   **C** | **C** | **C** | **Asus⁴** ‖
As he faced the sun he cast no shadow.

Verse 2   As Verse 1

Chorus 2
```
G              Asus⁴          C    | Em   D |
As they took his soul they stole his pride,
G              Asus⁴          C    | Em   D |
As they took his soul they stole his pride,
G              Asus⁴          C    | Em   D |
As they took his soul they stole his pride,
G              Asus⁴          C    | Em   D |
As they took his soul they took his pride.
```

Outro
```
Em           D      C        | C      |
As he faced the sun he cast no shadow,
Em           D      C        | C      |
As he faced the sun he cast no shadow,
Em           D      C        | C      |
As he faced the sun he cast no shadow,
Em           D      C        | C      |
As he faced the sun he cast no shadow.
```

```
| C    | C    | C    | G    ‖
```

Cigarettes And Alcohol

Words & Music by
Noel Gallagher

E5   F#   A5   F#7add11   Dsus2   A   Cadd9   B7

Intro

| E5 | E5 | E5 | E5 | E5 | E5 |

| F# | A5 | E5 | E5 | E5 | E5 ‖

Verse 1

    E5
Is it my imagination
        F#7add11   A5   E5 | E5 | E5 | E5 |
Or have I finally found something worth living for?
    E5
I was looking for some action
     F#7add11   A5   E5 | E5 | E5 | E5 ‖
But all I found was cigarettes and alcohol.

Bridge 1

   A5   E5
You could wait for a lifetime
   A5   E5
To spend your days in the sunshine,
   A5   E5
You might as well do the white-line.
            Dsus2   A
'Cause when it comes on top:

Chorus 1

                  E5   Dsus2
You gotta make it happen,
          A   E5   Dsus2
You gotta make it happen,
          A   E5   Dsus2
You gotta make it happen,
          A   E5 | Dsus2 A | Cadd9 | B7 ‖
You gotta make it happen.

Instrumental

| E5 | E5 | E5 | E5 | E5 | E5 |

| F# | A5 | E5 | E5 | E5 | E5 ‖

Verse 2

E5
Is it worth the aggravation

F#7add11
To find yourself a job

A5   E5 | E5 | E5 | E5 |
When there' nothing worth working for?

E5
It's a crazy situation,

F#7add11   A5   E5 | E5 | E5 | E5   ‖
But all I need are cigarettes and alcohol.

Bridge 2   As Bridge 1

Chorus 2   As Chorus 1

Instrumental   ‖: E5 | Dsus2 A | E5 | Dsus2 A :‖

E5   Dsus2   A
You gotta, you gotta, you gotta make it,
E5   Dsus2   A
You gotta, you gotta, you gotta fake it.
E5   Dsus2   A
You gotta, you gotta, you gotta make it,
E5   Dsus2   A
You gotta, you gotta, you gotta fake it.

Play 4 times

Guitar solo   ‖: E5 | Dsus2 A | E5 | Dsus2 A :‖ E5   ‖

Digsy's Dinner

Words & Music by
Noel Gallagher

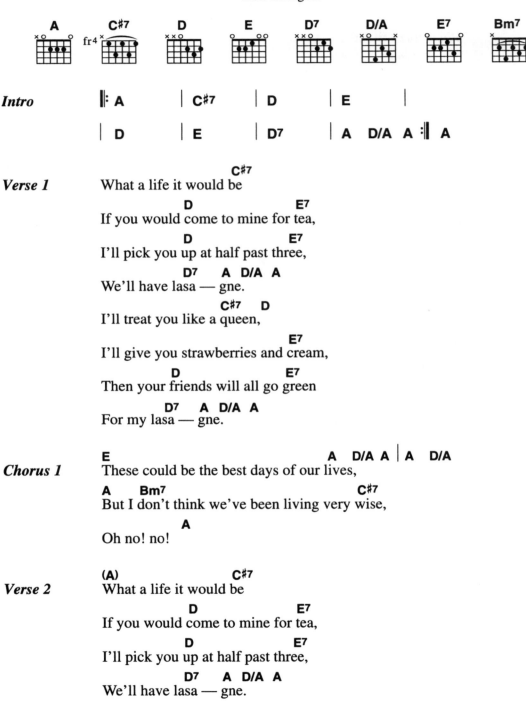

Intro

| : A | C#7 | D | E | |
| D | E | D7 | A D/A A : | A |

Verse 1

          C#7
What a life it would be
      D   E7
If you would come to mine for tea,
      D   E7
I'll pick you up at half past three,
        D7 A D/A A
We'll have lasa — gne.
        C#7 D
I'll treat you like a queen,
             E7
I'll give you strawberries and cream,
      D   E7
Then your friends will all go green
        D7 A D/A A
For my lasa — gne.

Chorus 1

  E   A D/A A | A D/A
These could be the best days of our lives,
  A Bm7   C#7
But I don't think we've been living very wise,
      A
Oh no! no!

Verse 2

  (A)   C#7
What a life it would be
      D   E7
If you would come to mine for tea,
      D   E7
I'll pick you up at half past three,
        D7 A D/A A
We'll have lasa — gne.

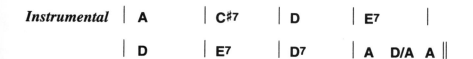

Instrumental | A | C#7 | D | E7 | |

| D | E7 | D7 | A D/A A ‖

Chorus 2   As Chorus 1

Verse 3
                 (A)   **C#7**
                 What a life it would be
                              D   **E7**
                 If you would come to mine for tea,
                              D   **E7**
                 I'll pick you up at half past three,
                              D7   **A D/A A**
                 We'll have lasa — gne.
                                          C#7   **D**
                 I'll treat you like a queen,
                                                E
                 I'll give you strawberries and cream,
                              D   **E**
                 Then your friends will all go green,
                              D   **E**
                 Then your friends will all go green,
                              D   **E**
                 Then your friends will all go green
                              D7   **A**
                 For my lasa — gne.

Don't Look Back In Anger

Words & Music by
Noel Gallagher

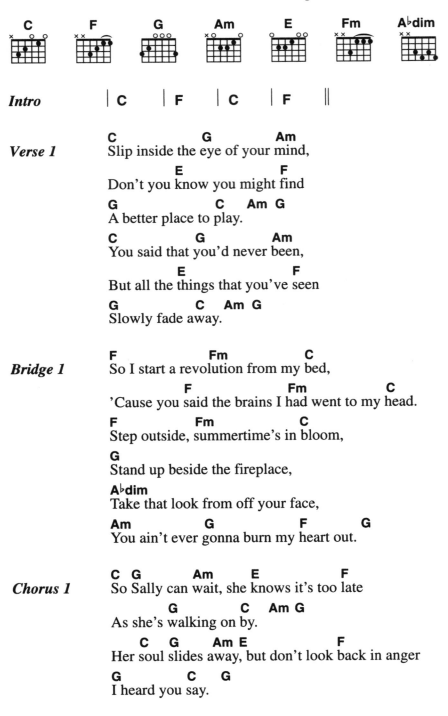

Intro ‖ C | F | C | F ‖

Verse 1

    C   G   Am
Slip inside the eye of your mind,
          E   F
Don't you know you might find
G   C   Am G
A better place to play.
    C   G   Am
You said that you'd never been,
          E   F
But all the things that you've seen
G   C   Am G
Slowly fade away.

Bridge 1

F   Fm   C
So I start a revolution from my bed,
        F   Fm   C
'Cause you said the brains I had went to my head.
F   Fm   C
Step outside, summertime's in bloom,
G
Stand up beside the fireplace,
A♭dim
Take that look from off your face,
Am   G   F   G
You ain't ever gonna burn my heart out.

Chorus 1

C G   Am   E   F
So Sally can wait, she knows it's too late
          G   C   Am G
As she's walking on by.
    C   G   Am E   F
Her soul slides away, but don't look back in anger
G   C G
I heard you say.

Instrumental | Am   E | F   G | C   Am   G ‖

Verse 2

    C   G   Am
Take me to the place where you go,

           E   F
Where nobody knows

G   C   Am   G
If it's night or day.

    C   G   Am
Please don't put your life in the hands

        E   F
Of a rock 'n' roll band

G   C   Am   G
Who'll throw it all away.

Bridge 2   As Bridge 1

Chorus 2

C   G   Am   E   F
So Sally can wait, she knows it's too late

           G   C   Am   G
As she's walking on by.

      C   G   Am   E   F
Her soul slides away, but don't look back in anger

G   C   Am   G
I heard you say.

Guitar solo   Chords as Bridge

Chorus 3   As Chorus 2

Chorus 4

C   G   Am   E   F
So Sally can wait, she knows it's too late

           G   C   Am   G
As she's walking on by.

      C   G   Am   Fadd9
Her soul slides away, but don't look back in anger,

       Fm7
Don't look back in anger

               C   G | Am   E | F   Fm |
I heard you say.

        C
It's not too late.

Live Forever

Words & Music by
Noel Gallagher

| G | D | Am7 | C | Em7 | Fsus2 |

Verse 1

G   D
Maybe I don't really want to know

      Am7
How your garden grows,

C   D
I just want to fly.

G   D
Lately, did you ever feel the pain

      Am7
In the morning rain

      C   D   Em7
As it soaks you to the bone.

Chorus 1

              D
Maybe I just want to fly,

              Am7
I want to live, I don't want to die,

           C
Maybe I just want to breathe,

      D   Em7
Maybe I just don't believe.

              D
Maybe you're the same as me,

             Am7
We see things they'll never see,

             Fsus2
You and I are gonna live forever.

Verse 2

        G   **D**
I said maybe really I don't want to know
           Am⁷
How your garden grows,
C   **D**
I just want to fly.
G   **D**
Lately, did you ever feel the pain
        Am⁷
In the morning rain
      C   **D**   **Em⁷**
As it soaks you to the bone.

Chorus 2

                D
Maybe I will never be
             Am⁷
All the things I want to be,
            C
But now is not the time to cry,
      D   **Em⁷**
Now's the time to find out why
          D
I think you're the same as me,
          Am⁷
We see things they'll never see,
         Fsus²
You and I are gonna live forever.

Guitar solo   Chords as Verse 1 and Chorus 1

Verse 3   As Verse 1

Chorus 3   As Chorus 1

      Am⁷   **Fsus²**
‖: Gonna live forever. :‖ *Play 6 times*

          Play 8 times
Guitar solo ‖: **Am⁷** | **Fsus²** :‖ **Am⁷** ‖

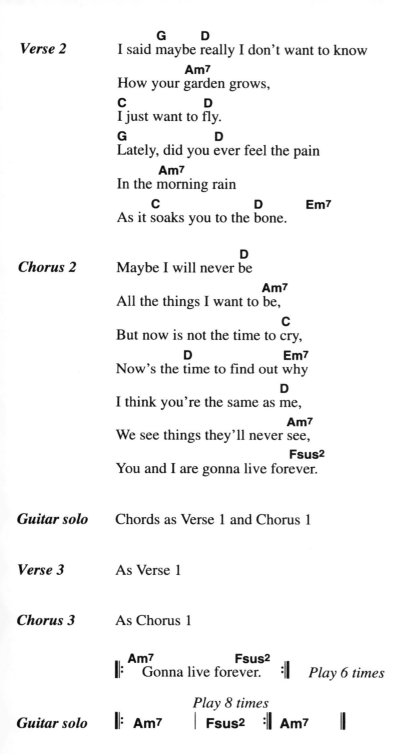

Married With Children

Words & Music by
Noel Gallagher

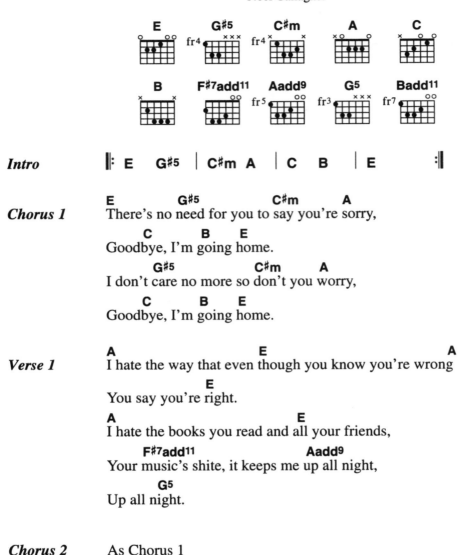

Intro

‖: E   G#5 | C#m A | C   B | E   :‖

Chorus 1

E　　　　G#5　　　　C#m　　　A
There's no need for you to say you're sorry,

　　　　C　　　B　　　E
Goodbye, I'm going home.

　　　　G#5　　　　　　C#m　　　A
I don't care no more so don't you worry,

　　　　C　　　B　　　E
Goodbye, I'm going home.

Verse 1

A　　　　　　　　　　　　　E　　　　　　　　　A
I hate the way that even though you know you're wrong

　　　　　　　　　E
You say you're right.

A　　　　　　　　　　　　E
I hate the books you read and all your friends,

　　F#7add11　　　　　　　　　Aadd9
Your music's shite, it keeps me up all night,

　　　　G5
Up all night.

Chorus 2　　　As Chorus 1

Verse 2

     A   E
I hate the way that you are so sarcastic,

       A   E
And you're not very bright.

A   E
You think that everything you've done's fantastic,

     F#7add11   Aadd9
Your music's shite, it keeps me up all night,

       G5
Up all night.

Guitar solo   ‖: E   G#5 | C#m A | C   B | E   :‖

Middle

C#m   G#5   Aadd9
And it will be nice to be alone

                    E
For a week or two.

C#m   G#5
But I know then I will be right,

Aadd9   Badd11
Right back here with you.

       Aadd9   G#5
With you,   with you,

       F#7add11   Badd11
With you,   with you,

       Aadd9   G#5   F#7add11
With you,   with you.

Chorus 3   As Chorus 1

Morning Glory

Words & Music by
Noel Gallagher

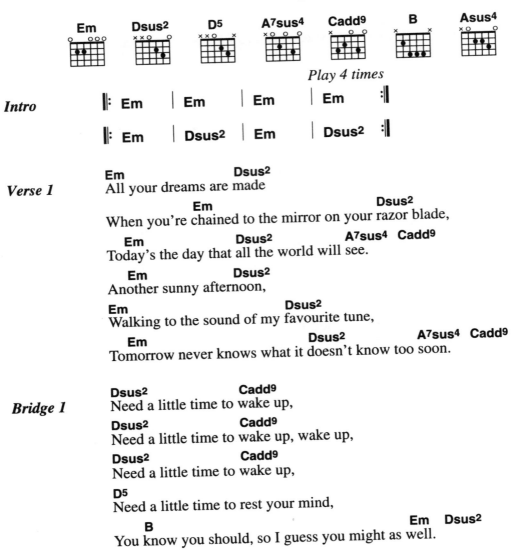

Play 4 times

Intro

‖: Em | Em | Em | Em :‖

‖: Em | Dsus² | Em | Dsus² :‖

Verse 1

Em   Dsus²
All your dreams are made

          Em   Dsus²
When you're chained to the mirror on your razor blade,

Em   Dsus²   A⁷sus⁴ Cadd⁹
Today's the day that all the world will see.

    Em   Dsus²
Another sunny afternoon,

Em   Dsus²
Walking to the sound of my favourite tune,

    Em   Dsus²   A⁷sus⁴ Cadd⁹
Tomorrow never knows what it doesn't know too soon.

Bridge 1

Dsus²   Cadd⁹
Need a little time to wake up,

Dsus²   Cadd⁹
Need a little time to wake up, wake up,

Dsus²   Cadd⁹
Need a little time to wake up,

D⁵
Need a little time to rest your mind,

     B   Em   Dsus²
You know you should, so I guess you might as well.

Chorus 1	**Asus4** **Cadd9** What's the story, Morning Glory?
	Em **Dsus2** **Asus4** **Cadd9** Well, you need a little time to wake up, wake up,
	Em **Dsus2** **Asus4** **Cadd9** Well, what's the story, Morning Glory?
	Em **Dsus2** **Asus4** **Cadd9** Well, you need a little time to wake up, wake up.

Chorus 1

Asus4   **Cadd9**
What's the story, Morning Glory?

Em **Dsus2**   **Asus4**   **Cadd9**
Well,   you need a little time to wake up, wake up,

Em **Dsus2** **Asus4**   **Cadd9**
Well,   what's the story, Morning Glory?

Em **Dsus2**   **Asus4**   **Cadd9**
Well,   you need a little time to wake up, wake up.

Instrumental

Play 4 times

‖: **Em** | **Em** | **Em** | **Em** :‖

‖: **Em** | **Dsus2** | **Em** | **Dsus2** :‖

Verse 3   As Verse 1

Bridge 2   As Bridge 1

Chorus 2   As Chorus 1

Chorus 3   As Chorus 1

Outro   ‖: **Em** | **Dsus2** | **Em** | **Dsus2** :‖ *Repeat to fade*

Rock 'n' Roll Star

Words & Music by
Noel Gallagher

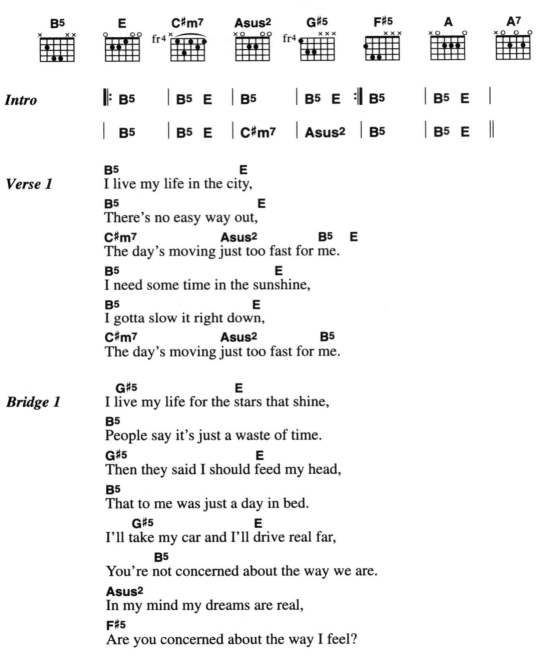

Intro

‖: B5 | B5 E | B5 | B5 E :‖ B5 | B5 E |

| B5 | B5 E | C♯m7 | Asus2 | B5 | B5 E ‖

Verse 1

B5   E
I live my life in the city,

B5   E
There's no easy way out,

C♯m7   Asus2   B5   E
The day's moving just too fast for me.

B5   E
I need some time in the sunshine,

B5   E
I gotta slow it right down,

C♯m7   Asus2   B5
The day's moving just too fast for me.

Bridge 1

G♯5   E
I live my life for the stars that shine,

B5
People say it's just a waste of time.

G♯5   E
Then they said I should feed my head,

B5
That to me was just a day in bed.

G♯5   E
I'll take my car and I'll drive real far,

B5
You're not concerned about the way we are.

Asus2
In my mind my dreams are real,

F♯5
Are you concerned about the way I feel?

Chorus 1

    Asus² E   **B5**
Tonight   I'm a rock 'n' roll star,

    Asus² E   **B5**
Tonight   I'm a rock 'n' roll star.

Verse 2   As Verse 1

Bridge 2   As Bridge 1

Chorus 2

    Asus² E   **B5**
Tonight   I'm a rock 'n' roll star,

    Asus² E   **B5**
Tonight   I'm a rock 'n' roll star,

    Asus² E   **B5**
Tonight   I'm a rock 'n' roll star.

Middle

Asus²
You're not down with who I am,

E   **B5**
Look at you now, you're all in my hands tonight.

Guitar solo   Chords as Verse 1

Chorus 3   As Chorus 2

Guitar solo

‖: A A7 | A A7 | A A7 | A A7 :‖

‖: F♯5 | E | F♯5 | E :‖

Outro

(E)   **F♯5 E**
It's just rock 'n' roll,

F♯5   **E**   **F♯5 E**
It's just rock 'n' roll,

F♯5   **E**   **F♯5 E**
It's just rock 'n' roll,

F♯5   **E**   **F♯5 E**
It's just rock 'n' roll,

F♯5   **E**   **F♯5 E**
It's just rock 'n' roll.

Repeat Outro ad lib. to fade

Roll With It

Words & Music by
Noel Gallagher

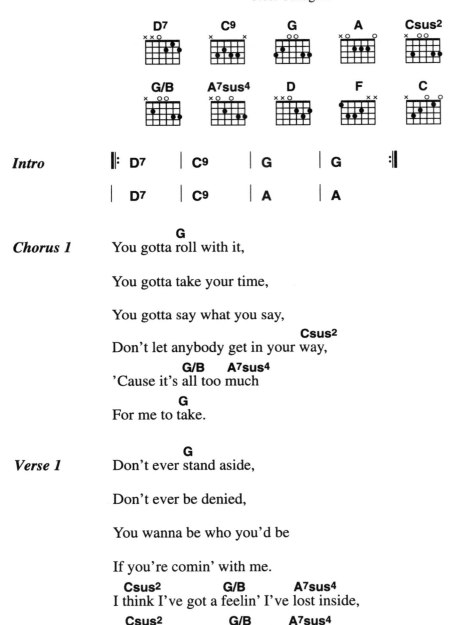

Intro   ‖: D7 | C9 | G | G :‖

| D7 | C9 | A | A

Chorus 1

      G
You gotta roll with it,

You gotta take your time,

You gotta say what you say,
                            Csus2
Don't let anybody get in your way,
          G/B   **A7sus4**
'Cause it's all too much
     G
For me to take.

Verse 1

          G
Don't ever stand aside,

Don't ever be denied,

You wanna be who you'd be

If you're comin' with me.
  Csus2   **G/B**   **A7sus4**
I think I've got a feelin' I've lost inside,
  Csus2   **G/B**   **A7sus4**
I think I'm gonna take me away and hide,
  Csus2 **G/B**   **D**   **G**
I'm thinkin' of things that I just can't abide.

Bridge 1

     F   G

I know the roads down which your life will drive,

     F   G

I'll find the key that lets you slip inside.

     F   G

Kiss the girl, she's not behind the door,

                F

But you know I think I recognise your face,

            C   D

But I've never seen you before.

Chorus 2   As Chorus 1

Guitar solo | G | G | G | G | Csus2 G/B | A7sus4 |

                    | Csus2 G/B | A7sus4 | Csus2 G/B | D | G | G ||

Bridge 2   As Bridge 1

Chorus 3   As Chorus 1

Verse 2

                    G

Don't ever stand aside,

Don't ever be denied,

You wanna be who you'd be

If you're comin' with me.

Coda

        Csus2   G/B   A7sus4

‖: I think I've got a feelin' I've lost inside,

        Csus2   G/B   A7sus4

I think I've got a feelin' I've lost inside,

        Csus2   G/B   A7sus4

I think I've got a feelin' I've lost inside,

        Csus2   G/B   A7sus4

I think I've got a feelin' I've lost inside. :‖

Play 3 times

Outro ‖: Csus2 G/B | A7sus4 :‖ G   ‖

Shakermaker

Words & Music by
Noel Gallagher

Chord diagrams: B7   B7add11   E7 (fr6)   Asus2   E   A   F#   D

Intro

| B7 | B7 | B7 | B7add11 | E7 | E7 |

| B7 | B7 | Asus2 | E | B7 | F# |

Verse 1

B7
I'd like to be somebody else,

And not know where I've been.
E7
I'd like to build myself a house
B7
Out of plasticine.

Chorus 1

A E   B7
Ah,___ shake along with me,
A E   B7   F#
Ah,___ shake along with me.

Verse 2

B7
I've been driving in my car,

With my friend Mr. Soft.
E7
Mr. Clean and Mr. Ben
B7
Are living in my loft.

Chorus 2   As Chorus 1

Guitar solo

| B7 | B7 | B7 | B7 | E7 | E7 |

| B7 | B7 | A | E | B7 | F# ||

Middle

     D   **A**   **B7**
I'm sorry but I just don't know,

    D   **A**   **B7**
I know you said I told you so.

             D   **A**   **B7**
But when you're happy and you're feeling fine,

              A   **E**
Then you'll know that it's the right time,

              A   **E**
Yeah you'll know that it's the wrong time:

     B7
To shake along with me,

     B7add11
Shake along with me,

    E7
Shake along with me,

     B7add11 | **Asus2** | **E** | **B7** | **F♯** ||
Shake along with me.

Verse 3

B7
Mr. Sifter sold me songs

When I was just sixteen.
E7
Now he stops at traffic lights
    B7
But only when they're green.

Chorus 3

‖: **A** **E**   **B7**
  Ah,___ shake along with me,
A **E**   **B7**
Ah,___ shake along with me. :‖

‖:   **B7**
  Shake along with me,
      B7add11
Shake along with me. :‖ *Play 4 times*

Instrumental | **B7** | **B7** | **B7** | **B7** | **E**   ‖

She's Electric

Words & Music by
Noel Gallagher

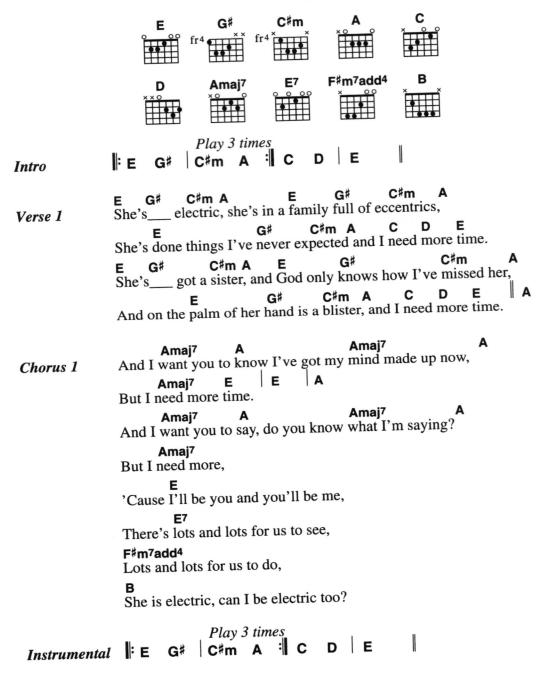

Intro

Play 3 times

|: E   G# | C#m   A :|| C   D | E ||

Verse 1

E   G#   C#m A   E   G#   C#m   A
She's___ electric, she's in a family full of eccentrics,
        E   G#   C#m A   C   D   E
She's done things I've never expected and I need more time.
E   G#   C#m A   E   G#   C#m   A
She's___ got a sister, and God only knows how I've missed her,
           E   G#   C#m A   C   D   E || A
And on the palm of her hand is a blister, and I need more time.

Chorus 1

    Amaj7   A   Amaj7   A
And I want you to know I've got my mind made up now,
    Amaj7   E | E | A
But I need more time.
    Amaj7   A   Amaj7   A
And I want you to say, do you know what I'm saying?
    Amaj7
But I need more,
        E
'Cause I'll be you and you'll be me,
        E7
There's lots and lots for us to see,
F#m7add4
Lots and lots for us to do,
B
She is electric, can I be electric too?

Instrumental

Play 3 times

|: E   G# | C#m   A :|| C   D | E ||

Verse 2

```
         E   G#        C#m  A    E            G#          C#m     A
She's___ got a brother, we don't get on with one another,
            E   G#        C#m  A    C    D       E
But I quite fancy her mother, and I think she likes me.
         E   G#        C#m  A   E           G#          C#m      A
She's___ got a cousin in fact she's got 'bout a dozen,
         E           G#        C#m  A    C       D     E       ‖ A
She's got one in the oven, but it's nothing to do with me.
```

Chorus 2

```
          Amaj7        A              Amaj7                 A
And I want you to know I've got my mind made up now,
          Amaj7     E   │ E     │ A
But I need more time.
          Amaj7        A              Amaj7                A
And I want you to say, do you know what I'm saying?
          Amaj7
But I need more,
              E
'Cause I'll be you and you'll be me,
              E7
There's lots and lots for us to see,
F#m7add4
Lots and lots for us to do,
B                               C   D │ E    │ C   D
She is electric, can I be electric too?
```

Outro

```
             E              C   D │ E    │ C   D
Can I be electric too?
             E              C   D │ E    │ C   D
Can I be electric too?
             E              C   D │ E    │
Can I be electric too?
C       │ D      │ E      │ E      ‖
Ah._____
```

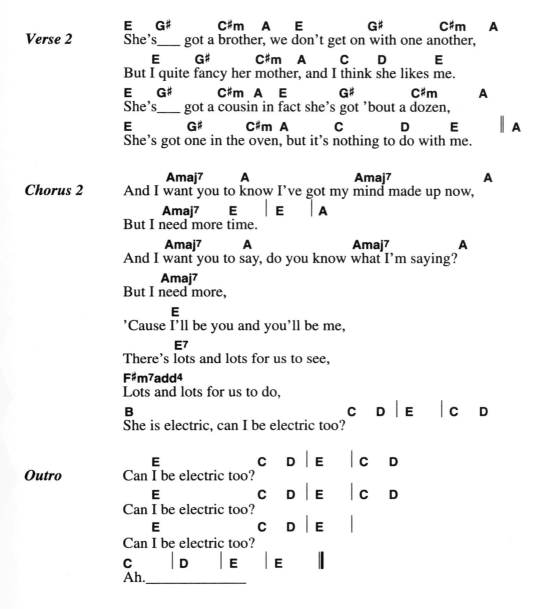

Slide Away

Words & Music by
Noel Gallagher

Am⁷   G   Fmaj⁹   Fadd⁹   G⁷   C   D⁷   E

Intro   ‖: Am⁷ | G Fmaj⁹ | Am⁷ | G Fmaj⁹ :‖

Verse 1
Am⁷   G   Fmaj⁹
Slide away and give it all you've got,
Am⁷   G   Fmaj⁹
My today fell in from the top.
    Am⁷   G   Fmaj⁹
I dream of you and all the things you say,
    Am⁷   G   Fmaj⁹
I wonder where you are now?

Verse 2
    Am⁷   G   Fmaj⁹
Hold me now all the world's asleep,
    Am⁷   G   Fmaj⁹
I need you now, you've knocked me off my feet.
    Am⁷   G   Fmaj⁹
I dream of you, we talk of growing old
Am⁷   G   Fmaj⁹
But you said please don't.

Bridge 1
    G   Fadd⁹
Slide in baby,
      G   Fadd⁹
Together we'll fly,
G   Fadd⁹
I tried praying,
     G   G⁷
But I don't know what you're saying to me.

Chorus 1

           C   G   Fmaj9
Now that you're mine we'll find a way of chasing the sun.
           Am7   G
Let me be the one that shines with you
         D7   Fmaj9
In the morning when you don't know what to do.
            C   G   Fmaj9
Two of a kind, we'll find a way to do what we've done.
           Am7   G
Let me be the one that shines with you,
               Fmaj9   D7
And we can slide away,
        Fmaj9 D7   Fmaj9 D7 G | E ||
Slide away,   slide away,   away.

Guitar solo   Chords as Verse 1 and Bridge 1

Verse 3   As Verse 1

Bridge 2
    G   Fadd9
Slide in baby,
      G   Fadd9
Together we'll fly,
    G   Fadd9
I've tried praying,
      G   G7
And I know just what you're saying to me.

Chorus 2

            C   G   Fmaj9
Now that you're mine we'll find a way of chasing the sun.
           Am7   G
Let me be the one that shines with you
         D7   Fmaj9
In the morning when you don't know what to do.
            C   G   Fmaj9
Two of a kind, we'll find a way to do what we've done.
           Am7   G
Let me be the one that shines with you,
               Fmaj9   D7
And we can slide away,
        Fmaj9 D7   Fmaj9
Slide away,   slide away,
    D7   Fmaj9 D7   Fmaj9
‖:   Slide away,   slide away. :‖   *Repeat ad lib. to fade*

Some Might Say

Words & Music by
Noel Gallagher

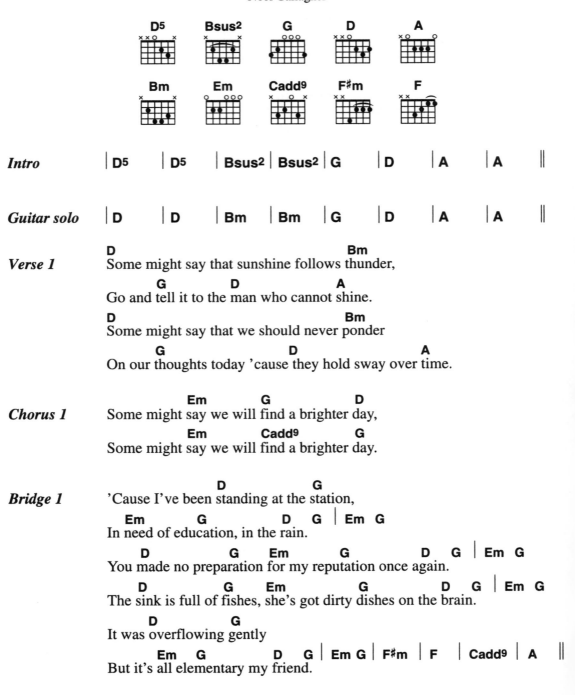

Intro

| D5 | D5 | Bsus2 | Bsus2 | G | D | A | A ||

Guitar solo

| D | D | Bm | Bm | G | D | A | A ||

Verse 1

D   Bm
Some might say that sunshine follows thunder,
    G   D   A
Go and tell it to the man who cannot shine.
D   Bm
Some might say that we should never ponder
    G   D   A
On our thoughts today 'cause they hold sway over time.

Chorus 1

                    Em   G   D
Some might say we will find a brighter day,
                    Em   Cadd9   G
Some might say we will find a brighter day.

Bridge 1

                    D   G
'Cause I've been standing at the station,
    Em   G   D   G | Em G
In need of education, in the rain.
    D   G   Em   G   D   G | Em G
You made no preparation for my reputation once again.
    D   G   Em   G   D   G | Em G
The sink is full of fishes, she's got dirty dishes on the brain.
    D   G
It was overflowing gently
    Em   G   D   G | Em G | F#m | F | Cadd9 | A ||
But it's all elementary my friend.

Guitar solo | D | D | Bm | Bm |

| G | D | A | A ||

Verse 2

D   Bm
Some might say they don't believe in heaven,
          G   D   A
Go and tell it to the man who lives in hell.
D   Bm
Some might say you get what you've been given,
          G   D   G
If you don't get yours I won't get mine as well.

Chorus 2   As Chorus 1

Bridge 2

(G)   D   G
'Cause I've been standing at the station,
    Em   G   D   G | Em G
In need of education, in the rain.
              D   G   Em   G   D   G | Em G
You made no preparation for my reputation once again.
            D   G   Em   G   D   G | Em G
The sink is full of fishes, she's got dirty dishes on the brain.
D   G
How my dog's been itchin',
Em   G   D   G | Em G
Itchin' in the kitchen once again.

Outro

G   D   G | Em
Some might say,
G   D   G | Em
Some might say,
||: (Em)   G   D   G | Em
    You know some might say,
          G   D   G | Em
You know some might say.   :||

Repeat to fade

Supersonic

Words & Music by
Noel Gallagher

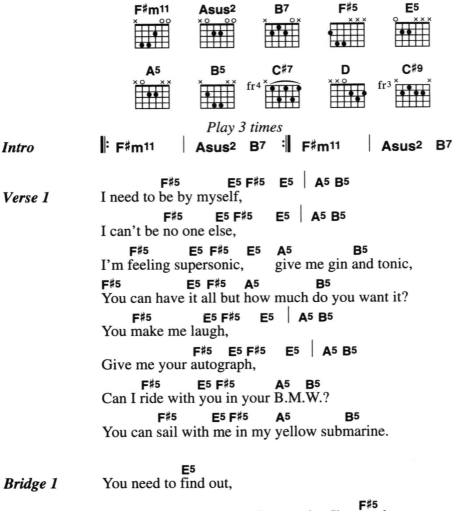

Play 3 times

Intro   𝄆 F#m11 | Asus2 B7 𝄇 F#m11 | Asus2 B7

Verse 1
　　　　　 F#5　　 E5 F#5　 E5 | A5 B5
I need to be by myself,
　　　　　 F#5　　 E5 F#5　　 E5 | A5 B5
I can't be no one else,
　　　 F#5　　　 E5 F#5　 E5　 A5　　　　 B5
I'm feeling supersonic,　　 give me gin and tonic,
F#5　　　　 E5 F#5　 A5　　　　 B5
You can have it all but how much do you want it?
　　 F#5　　　　 E5 F#5　 E5 | A5 B5
You make me laugh,
　　　　　　 F#5　 E5 F#5　 E5 | A5 B5
Give me your autograph,
　　 F#5　　　 E5 F#5　　 A5　 B5
Can I ride with you in your B.M.W.?
　　　　　 F#5　　 E5 F#5　 A5　　　　 B5
You can sail with me in my yellow submarine.

Bridge 1
　　　　　　 E5
You need to find out,
　　　　　　　　　　　　　　 F#5
'Cause no one's gonna tell you what I'm on about.
　　　 E5
You need to find a way,
　　　　　　　　　 C#7
For what you want to say, but before tomorrow.

Chorus 1

        D   **A5**   **E5**   **F#5**
'Cause my friend said he'd take you home,

       D   **A5**   **E5**   **F#5**
He sits in a corner all alone.

D   **A5**   **E5**   **F#5**
He lives under a waterfall,

D   **A5**
Nobody can see him,

E5   **F#5**   **D**   **A5**
Nobody can ever hear him call,

E5   **F#5**   **D**   **A5**
Nobody can ever hear him call.

Guitar solo

| **E5** **F#5** | **D** **A5** | **E5** **F#5** | **D** **A5** |

| **E5** **F#5** | **E5** | **E5** | **C#9** | **C#9** |

Verse 2

          F#5   **E5 F#5**   **E5** | **A5 B5**
You need to be yourself,

          F#5   **E5 F#5**   **E5** | **A5 B5**
You can't be no one else.

  F#5   **E5**   **F#5 E5**   **A5**   **B5**
I know a girl called Elsa, she's into Alka Seltzer,

    F#5   **E5 F#5**   **A5**   **B5**
She sniffs it through a cane on a supersonic train.

       F#5   **E5 F#5** **E5** | **A5 B5**
And she makes me laugh,

        F#5 **E5 F#5**   **E5** | **A5 B5**
I got her autograph.

     F#5   **E5 F#5** **E5 A5**   **B5**
She's done it with a doctor   on a helicopter,

     F#5   **E5 F#5**   **E5 A5**   **B5**
She's sniffin' in her tissue, sellin' the big issue.

Bridge 2

        E5
When she finds out,

                                    F#5
'Cause no ones's gonna tell her what I'm on about.

        E5
You need to find a way

            C#7
For what you want to say, but before tomorrow.

Continued on next page...

Chorus 2

          D   **A5**   **E5**   **F♯5**
'Cause my friend said he'd take you home,

      D   **A5**   **E5**   **F♯5**
He sits in a corner all alone.

D   **A5**   **E5**   **F♯5**
He lives under a waterfall,

D   **A5**
Nobody can see him,

E5   **F♯5**   **D**   **A5**
Nobody can ever hear him call,

E5   **F♯5**   **D**   **A5**
Nobody can ever hear him call.

Guitar solo   ‖: **E5** **F♯5** | **D**   **A5** :‖   *Repeat to fade*

Hey Now

Words & Music by
Noel Gallagher

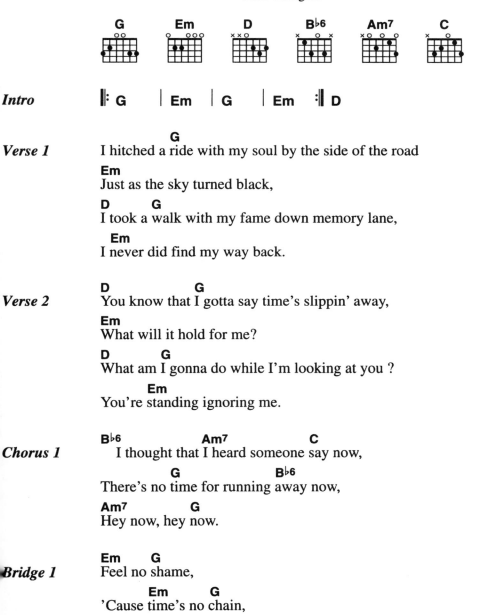

Intro   ‖: G | Em | G | Em :‖ D

Verse 1
         G
I hitched a ride with my soul by the side of the road
Em
Just as the sky turned black,
D   **G**
I took a walk with my fame down memory lane,
    Em
I never did find my way back.

Verse 2
    D   **G**
You know that I gotta say time's slippin' away,
Em
What will it hold for me?
D   **G**
What am I gonna do while I'm looking at you ?
    Em
You're standing ignoring me.

Chorus 1
B♭6   **Am7**   **C**
  I thought that I heard someone say now,
      G   **B♭6**
There's no time for running away now,
Am7   **G**
Hey now, hey now.

Bridge 1
Em **G**
Feel no shame,
    Em   **G**
'Cause time's no chain,
Em **G**   **Em** **D**
Feel no shame.

Verse 3

        G
The first thing I saw, as I walked through the door,

        Em
Was a sign on the wall that read.

D   **G**
It said "You might never know that I want you to know

        Em   **D**
What's written inside of your head"

Verse 4

        G
And time as it stands won't be held in my hands

        Em
Or living inside of my skin.

D   **G**
And as it fell from the sky I asked myself why,

        Em
Can I never let anyone in?

Chorus 2

B♭6   **Am7**   **C**
  I thought that I heard someone say now,

        G   **B♭6**
There's no time for running away now,

Am7   **G**
Hey now, hey now.

Bridge 2

Em   **G**
Feel no shame,

        Em   **G**
'Cause time's no chain,

Em   **G**   **Em**   **D**
Feel no shame.

Guitar solo   Chords as Verse and Chorus

Bridge 3   As Bridge 1

Verse 5   As Verse 1

Verse 6   As Verse 2

B♭6   **Am7**   **C**
I thought that I heard someone say now,

     G   **B♭6**
There's no time for running away now,

Am7   **C**   **G**
Hey now, hey now, hey now,

B♭6   **Am7**   **C**   **G**
Hey now, hey now, hey now, hey now,

B♭6   **Am7**   **G**
Hey now, hey now, hey now.

Em   **G**
Feel no shame

     Em   **G**
'Cause time's no chain.

Em   **G**
Feel no shame

     Em   **G**
'Cause time's no chain.

Repeat Bridge 4 to fade

Up In The Sky

Words & Music by
Noel Gallagher

Intro

| G5 | G5 | G5 | G5 | G5 | G5 | Gsus4 | Gsus4 |

| Gadd#11 | Gsus4 | G5 | G5 | G5 ||

Verse 1

G5
Hey you! Up in the sky

Learning to fly, tell me how high

Fadd9   C
Do you think you'll go

G5
Before you start falling?

Hey you, up in a tree,

You wanna be me, well that couldn't be

Fadd9   C
'Cause the people here,

G5   C Csus4 C
They don't hear you calling.

A7   G5
How does it feel when you're inside me?

Verse 2

(G5)
Hey you! Wearing the crown,

Making no sound, I heard you feel down,

Fadd9   C
Well that's just too bad,

G5
Welcome to my world.

(G5)
Hey you! Stealing the light,

I heard that the shine's gone out of your life,
        Fadd9   **C**
Well that's just too bad,
        G5   **C Csus4 C**
Welcome to my world.
        A7   **G5**
How does it feel when you're inside me?

        D

Bridge 1   You'll need assistance with the things that you
        Em   **D** **C**
Have never ever seen,
        D
It's just a case of never breathing out
        Em   **D C A7**
Before you've breathed it in.
        C/D   **G5** | **G5** | **G5** | **G5** ‖
How does it feel when you're inside?

| **G5** | **G5** | **G5** |
        Gsus4   **Gadd♯11 Gsus4**
I can feel you, can you feel   me?

| **G5** | **G5** | **G5** | **G5** ‖

Verse 3   As Verse 1

Bridge 2   As Bridge 1

Instrumental | **G5** | **G5** | **G5** | **G5** |

‖: **G5** | **G5** | **G5** | **G5** |

| **Gsus4** | **Gsus4** | **Gadd♯11** | **Gsus4** :‖   *Repeat to fade*

Wonderwall

Words & Music by
Noel Gallagher

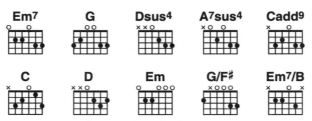

Use Capo at 2nd fret to play along with the recording

Intro   ‖: Em⁷ G │ Dsus⁴ │ A⁷sus⁴ │ Em⁷ G │ Dsus⁴ │ A⁷sus⁴ :‖

Verse 1

Em⁷   **G**
Today is gonna be the day

          Dsus⁴   **A⁷sus⁴**
That they're gonna throw it back to you,

Em⁷   **G**
By now you should have somehow

     Dsus⁴   **A⁷sus⁴**
Realised what you gotta do.

Em⁷   **G**   **Dsus⁴**   **A⁷sus⁴**
I don't believe that anybody feels the way that I do

        Cadd⁹ Dsus⁴ │ **A⁷sus⁴** ‖
About you now.

Verse 2

Em⁷   **G**
Back beat, the word is on the street

       Dsus⁴   **A⁷sus⁴**
That the fire in your heart is out,

Em⁷   **G**
I'm sure you've heard it all before,

       Dsus⁴   **A⁷sus⁴**
But you never really had a doubt.

Em⁷   **G**   **Dsus⁴**   **A⁷sus⁴**
I don't believe that anybody feels the way that I do

        Em⁷ G │ **Dsus⁴ A⁷sus⁴** ‖
About you now.

Bridge 1

      C   **D**   **Em**
And all the roads we have are winding,

      C   **D**   **Em**
And all the lights that lead us there are blinding,

C   **D**   **G**   **G/F♯** **Em**
There are many things that I would like to say to you

              A⁷sus⁴
But I don't know how.

Chorus 1

       Cadd⁹   **Em⁷** | **G**
Because maybe,

     Em⁷   **Cadd⁹**   **Em⁷** **G**
You're gonna be the one that saves me,

     Em⁷ Cadd⁹ **Em⁷** | **G**
And after all,

         Em⁷   **Cadd⁹** **Em⁷** | **G Em⁷/B** | **N.C. A⁷sus⁴** ‖
You're my wonderwall.

Verse 3

Em⁷   **G**
Today was gonna be the day,

     Dsus⁴   **A⁷sus⁴**
But they'll never throw it back at you,

Em⁷   **G**
By now you should have somehow

   Dsus⁴   **A⁷sus⁴**
Realised what you're not to do.

Em⁷   **G**   **Dsus⁴**   **A⁷sus⁴**
I don't believe that anybody feels the way I do

      Em⁷ G | **Dsus⁴ A⁷sus⁴** ‖
About you now.

Bridge 2

      C   **D**   **Em**
And all the roads that lead you there were winding,

      C   **D**   **Em**
And all the lights that light the way are blinding,

C   **D**   **G**   **G/F♯** **Em**
There are many things that I would like to say to you

              A⁷sus⁴
But I don't know how.

Continued on next page...

Chorus 2

         Cadd⁹   **Em⁷** | **G**
I said maybe

      Em⁷   **Cadd⁹**   **Em⁷** | **G**
You're gonna be the one that saves me

      Em⁷ Cadd⁹ **Em⁷** | **G**
And after all

            Em⁷   **Cadd⁹ Em⁷** | **G Em⁷** ‖
You're my wonderwall.

Chorus 3   As Chorus 2

Outro

         Cadd⁹   **Em⁷** | **G**
I said maybe

      Em⁷   **Cadd⁹**   **Em⁷** | **G**
You're gonna be the one that saves me,

      Em⁷   **Cadd⁹**   **Em⁷** | **G**
You're gonna be the one that saves me,

      Em⁷   **Cadd⁹**   **Em⁷** | **G Em⁷** ‖
You're gonna be the one that saves me.

Instrumental ‖: **Cadd⁹ Em⁷** | **G Em⁷** | **Cadd⁹ Em⁷** | **G Em⁷** :‖